The Unknown Reich

Perry Pierik

The Unknown Reich

Less Known Facts
of the Eastern Front

Aspekt 2014

THE UNKNOWN REICH
© Perry Pierik
© 2014 Publishing House ASPEKT
Amersfoortsestraat 27, 3769 AD Soesterberg, Nederland
info@uitgeverijaspekt.nl-http://www.uitgeverijaspekt.nl

Cover: Thomas Wunderink
Interlining: Thomas Wunderink
Translated by: Ellen van den Broek

ISBN: 9789461536433
NUR: 680

All rights reserved. No part of these pages, either text or image may be used for any purpose other than personal use. Therefore, reproduction, modification, storage in a retrieval system or retransmission, in any form or by any means, electronic, mechanical or otherwise, for reasons other than personal use, is strictly prohibited without prior written permission.

Table of Contents

Introduction	7
The Kommandostab Reichsführer-SS – an Unknown, but Murderous Branch of the SS' Empire	11
A Combination of Front Soldiers and Murderers	15
A Tainted Reputation	21
The Waffen-SS' Cavalry and the Jews of Tomsk	25
Motal	27
The Waffen-SS and the Fields of Corpses at Pinsk	31
Massacres between Rowno and Shitomir	37
The 1st SS-Brigade's (mot.) Common Front Work at Korosten	39
'Difficult but Necessary'	43
Compromising	51
Rückwärtiges Heeresgebietskommando – a Forgotten Chapter	55
Max von Schenckendorff, Karl von Roques, Franz von Roques and Erich Friderici	59
Sicherungsdivisionen	69
Bielsk and Vilnius – the Cooperation between Einsatzgruppen and Sicherungsdivisionen	73
The Battle for Jewish Possessions	75
Famine	79
Between Apathy and Revolt	81

The Losses of Soviet-tanks and the Remarkable Resemblance of Losses between 1941 and 1945	85
The Red Air Force – Astronomical Losses Throughout the War, However, the Industry was Spared	89
Czech Tanks for the Wehrmacht	105
The Battle of the Tanks at Rossieni	113
'Marder' and 'Hetzer'	119
Tensions with Guderian: Controversial Infantry-Cavalry	123
The 137th Infantry Division	129
Borodino	135
Desná-Jelnja Arch: 'The Infantry Barely Fought'	139
The Red Army's Unimaginative Performances: Daily Assaults and – Massacres	147
Works Cited	155

Introduction

In this book we highlight a number of unknown facets of the war in Russia. Operation 'Barbarossa', the German invasion of Russia, was the largest campaign during the Second World War. During this war a number of aspects have become very well-known, such as the battle for Stalingrad, the defense of Moscow, the siege of Sevastopol, and of course the Soviet contribution made to the liberation of Europe. However, much is unknown or gradually became less known. Some of these events are gathered in this work. We have tried to highlight several fields, from matters of political nature to military affairs.

First, we bring forward a quite unknown organization of the SS, which has done despicable things. To be precise, which is remarkable, it concerned a part of the Waffen-SS, the military branch of the SS, the so-called Kommandostab Reichsführer-SS. This unit was comprised of three brigades which were meant to strengthen

the Höhere SS und Polizeiführer's influence in occupied Russia. In addition they would strengthen Himmler's position opposed to the army and party. The brigades committed horrendous crimes during their deployment, partly in cooperation with the notorious Einsatzgruppen and sometimes with the army's Sicherungsdivisionen (security divisions in the areas behind the front).

These crimes are the reason we highlight the Rückwärtiges Heeresgebietskommando and its commanders: Max von Schenckendorff, Karl von Roques, Franz von Roques and Enrich Friderici. The continuous bordering of this organization and its commanders against the 'Holocaust of bullets' – the murders committed by the Einsatzgruppen – are an indication of the overlapping responsibilities and administrative chaos typical to the Third Reich. The Kommandostab 'in itself' was an example, as the 2nd Brigade served as the home base for the Dutch and Flemish Waffen-SS's Of all Units this one met the front quickly and avoided the mass murders to which the 1st brigade and the cavalry brigade of Hermann Fegelein rendered itself guilty. A small administrative decision determined who became murderers.

On military grounds we highlight the colossal losses at the eastern front. About this a number of remarkable things can be said, for example concerning the scale of losses between the start and the end of the war, where, for instance, tremendous Russian losses in 1945 are standing out. The war has obviously been brought to a quick halt by Stalin, for which man paid the price.

It is additionally interesting to discuss German armament efforts, such as the inclusion of the Czech weapon industry. Finally we highlight the tense relations between the motorized units and the infantry. In history a lot of attention has been paid to the 'Blitzkrieg' and the armored units. The 'workhorse' of the infantry, however, is sometimes left out of this discussion. Based on incidents at the 137th infantry division we highlight these complicated relations. It is a grasp of, what effortlessly could become a series of monographs, however it is still worth the effort and attention.

Perry Pierik.

The Kommandostab Reichsführer-SS – an Unknown, but Murderous Branch of the SS' Empire

History still struggles with the Holocaust. In Eastern-Europe many questions remain unanswered. One of them is how and to what extent the Waffen-SS were involved in war crimes in Eastern Europe. According to some, the

Himmler visiting his SS-riders at the Pripyat swamps

Waffen-SS was primarily an ordinary military organization which got caught up in the fights at the front. Others stated that the Waffen-SS was part of the SS' killing machine. The confusion surrounding this matter was primarily caused by a somewhat unknown organization of the SS: the Kommandostab Reichsführer-SS. This unit fulfilled an ambivalent as well as a criminal role during the war against the Soviet-Union.

The origin of the Kommandostab goes back to the summer of 1940, when Himmler uncovered Hitler's plans of a war against Russia. The SS wanted to continue the built of, what Albert Speer, Hitler's favorite architect and war production man, later described as 'the state of slaves'. The SS continuously left their mark on the Third Reich. Himmler had also set his eyes on the power area behind the front, the Korprückwärts (Korück), where he believed the influence of his 'regular' police units to be insufficient. Himmler created, with his Kommandostab, comprised of three brigades, a new body which stood between police and military affairs. This new body was deployed to strengthen the position of his direct executors, the several Höhere SS and Polizeiführer (HSSPF) with regards to the competition (the army). All this had come about because of experience gained during the Poland campaign, where the SS and the army had clashed on several occasions, mostly because of the deployment of the SS-Totenkopsverbände, selected from the SS-Wachmanschaft of the KZ's, and the competition between the armored branch of the SS, the Waffen-S, and the army.

The SS Cavalry Brigade's reconnaissance unit

Hitler gave Himmler's SS murder squads a free reign

A Combination of Front Soldiers and Murderers

With the establishment of the Kommandostab Reichsführer-SS, a strange combination between the military apparatus of the SS and the police unites of the SS (SD) had come about. Particularly the fact that the staff was

Waffen-SS cavalry and Soviet citizens who are suspected of being 'Heckenschützen'

part of the Waffen-SS, thus the military apparatus, strengthened this. The war crimes, which stemmed from the activities of the Kommandostab, would leave an everlasting stain on the reputation of the Waffen-SS.

On the eve of operation 'Barbarossa', the German invasion of the Soviet-Union in 1914, the SS and the Wehrmacht had come together in Graz on April 16,1941. The aim of the gathering was the authority of the captured areas. As long as there was war, the army should be considered the authoritative force, however, the gathering was additionally taking place to involve the SS. It was decided that the HSSPF would be 'beigeordnet' (added). As a result, tasks and responsibilities began to overlap, which was typical to Hitler-Germany. In general sense Hitler supported such initiatives because it would enable him to overrule underlying parties via authorization and to play them off against each other. Only five days after the meeting in Graz the entire plan was drawn up and the army caved. On May 21,1941 the plan was implemented, hardly a month before the invasion.

The new body itself had been established on April 7,1941 and was initially known as the Einsatzstab Reichsführer-SS. On May 6 of that same year, it was renamed the Kommandostab Reichsführer-SS. The commander became one of Hitler's confidants, the 45-year old SS-Brigadeführer Kurt Knoblauch, whose military

The involvement at the Pripyat swamps

The Unknown Reich

Kommissariaten in Eastern Europe

began in 1905, and who had served as companies-and battalion commander in the First World War. After the war, Knoblauch served in the Reichswehr, however, after his discharge he chose for a career in politics. Via functions within the SS-Hauptampt, the SS-Führungsamt and the division 'Totenkopf' he made a name for himself within the empire of the SS. Until 1943 Knoblauch would serve the Stab. His immediate right-hand was SS-Obersturmbannführer Fritz Freitag from East Prussia, who had given up his study in medicine because he had ended up with the SS after 1918 via a Freikorpscarrière. He had participated during the Poland campaign with the 3rd Polizeiregiment.

In April the actual establishment of the Kommandostab units began to take place. Organisationchef (Organizing officer) Hans Jüttner brought together SS-regiments for this purpose: The 4th, 8th, 10th, and cavalry units of the Waffen SS, which were encamped at the Generalgouvernement in Cracow. One already built body of command, the Befehlshaber Ost of the Waffen-SS, was transformed into the staff of the first brigade which originated from this initiative. Primarily the 1st SS Brigade (mot.) fell under the command of Karl-Maria Demelhuber. However, he was soon replaced by SS-Brigadeführer Richard Herrmann, who, because of his interest in sports, was known as 'Handball-Hermann' ('Dodge ball Hermann'). The 2nd SS Brigade (mot.) was established at Warsaw, and composed of the SS-regiments 4 and 14, which were brought in from the Netherlands towards Poland. The staff of the 2nd Brigade existed of the Dienstelle Nordwest, the body of staff of the Waffen-SS in The Hague, which was deconstructed afterwards. This brigade was placed under the command of SS-Brigadeführer Karl von Treuenfeld, who was quickly replaced by the former commander of the 4th: SS Inf-Rgt., SS-Oberführer Gottfried Klingmann. The rows were additionally reinforced with the Begleitbataillon Reichsführer-SS. This unit had been established in Oranienburg near Berlin and was placed under the command of SS-Sturmbannführer Schützeck. Aside from the other units, two SS-cavalry regiments served the Kommandostab Reichsführer-SS, who jointly formed the 1st SS Kav. Brigade. In all, more than 18.000 men served the Kommandostab, combined they had the force of a division.

A Tainted Reputation

Although the Kommandostab Reichsführer-SS had been established to operate behind the front, their deployment from June 22,1941 – the start of operation 'Barbarossa' – went beyond those borders. The unit had

'The one thing abundant here, are children',
the Waffen-SS dotted down after seeing this photo

been sorted into the XXXXII. Army corps as a back-up. However, they immediately made use of the troops. The 1st SS Kavallerieregiment was deployed in the area of the 87th Inf. Div, and units of the 8th SS Inf. Rgt. were deployed at Augustowo. Both regiments immediately committed war crimes. At first, at Augustowo, the execution of captured Jews took place under the command of the SD and Grenzpolizei from Sovetsk (also known as Tilsit), although the actual executions were carried out by the Kommandostab. However, this would change soon. The Kommandostab would, in the months to come, defile the reputation of the Waffen-SS forever by committing horrendous war crimes. Nevertheless the SS-Brigadeführer Knoblauch was praised by his army comrades after his first efforts with the XXXXII.

The Kommandostab Reichsführer-SS brigades have been forgotten by many historians. A recent study by historian Martin Cüppens has corrected this. However, to the management of the SS the Kommandostab Reichsführer played a vital role. It was for a reason that the headquarters of the SS-Cavalry brigade was placed at Lachowicze, close to the HSSPF Von dem Bach – Zelewski, who at Baranowicze, approximately 9 miles away, had placed his headquarters. The Reichsführer-SS Heinrich Himmler flew to Baranowicze (now known as Baranovichi) on July 31,1941 in order to witness the efforts of his unit. The brigades were on the verge of leaving behind a trail of blood in the backdrop of the HSSPF Hans-Adolf Prützmann (the Baltic States – 'Russland Nord'), Erich von dem Bach-Zeleweski ('Russland-Mitte' – which mainly covered Belarus), and Friedrich Jeckeln, 'Russland-Süd', which primarily concerned the Ukraine.

Erich von dem Bach-Zelewski

Heinrich Himmler

The Waffen-SS' Cavalry and the Jews of Tomsk

The cavalry operated in the area of 'Russland-Mitte'. The two regiments of the 1st SS Kavallerie Brigade operated seperately. The first regiment operated between the river the Bug and the Pripyat swamps, and in the early weeks

The Waffen-SS was welcomed with salt and bread at the Pripyat swamps

of the war the place of operations was the area south of Baranowicze: Antopal, Chiomsl, Tomsk, Motal, Telechany, Swieta, Wólka, and Hantsavichy. We learn of the regiments operations from the fate of the Jewish community at Tomsk, that contained around 2.000 citizens. Units of the 1st SS Kavallerieregiment, under the command of SS-Officer Gustav Lombard, arrived at Tomsk on August 2, 1941. Von dem Bach – Zeleweski knew, as HSSPF, what was about to happen as he reported to Himmler 'Judenaktion im Gange' (Jew action taking place).

In the meantime the Waffen-SS had dug a burial pit just outside of Tomsk and the next day the Jewish community was executed there. In his report Lombard wrote that Tomsk 'had been cleansed of all doubtful elements'. Historian Cüppers also mentioned that the locals covered the bodies in quicklime and buried them. It appeared that the locals were not really concerned with the fates of their fellow Jewish citizens, something which occurred frequently in the Ukraine. In the reports of the Einsatzgruppen it was often stated that anti-Jewish measures and murders took place with the consent of the population.

Motal

After Tomsk it was Motal's turn. It was on Friday after the Sabbath that the Germans forced their way in. The population was hunted down. Cüppers: 'The Germans forced their way into the house of the Jewish barber

The Waffen-SS cavalry at an entrenched Soviet-tank dome

Avraham Nun and found his wife, who had just gotten a miscarriage'. Because the woman was too weak to join the, over at the church collected Jews, she was shot on sight by the Waffen-SS. During this execution many Christians once again offered to help. Children were given candy in exchange for Jew hideaways. There were even Christian inhabitants who actively sought out Jews. 'A Belarusian, called Pinchok, found Menachem Tubianski who was trying to escape, and beat him to death with a stick. Another Christian citizen uncovered the trader Yitzchak Bagon with his wife and four kids. Bagon begged for his life and for that of his family, and even offered money which he carried on him. However, the inhabitant immediately reported the family to the Waffen-SS' cavalry. Because they disobeyed the order to remain at the church, the family was executed against the first garden wall they could find.'

Thirty Jewish men were deported from Motal and ordered to dig a mass grave, after which they were executed. The remainder of the masculine community was forced, while they were carrying the corpse of the barber's wife, to walk to the grave. The 800 men were told to lie face-down in the grave face after which they were shot. The local population helped close the grave. The next morning 2200 children and women were brought to an open field and shot with machine guns. After that Motal was sought through again. Anyone who was found was immediately killed. A Jew who had been able to hide after the first rounds of executions, was discovered by a Belarusian, handed over to the Germans, and murdered afterwards. However, not all inhabitants collaborated with the Waffen-SS. Farmers and several city inhabitants offered runaway Jews a place to stay.

To learn from Lombard of the progress that had been made, Von den Bach-Zelewski flew to the area with his Fieseler Storch plane. The Waffen-SS and the HSSPF and Kommandostab worked closely together. After the execution of 3000 Jews in Motal, operations in Telechany ('A bigger city of Jews' according to Lombard) took place on August 5, Swieta and Wólka between August 6 and 7, 1941, and Hantsavichy on August 11. According to official reports 6504 Jews were executed by the Waffen-SS cavalry. However, there are signs which state that the real number was significantly higher and added up to approximately 10.000 people. The Waffen-SS had not lost a single soul during this period of time, which is proof that these events should be seen as the simple executions of others, and not as fights against partisans.

Hans-Adolf Prützmann

The *Waffen-SS* and the Fields of Corpses at Pinsk

The situation was similar at the 2nd SS-Kavallerieregiment of the 1st SS-Kavallerie Brigade who, under the command of SS-Officer Franz Magill, originating from Pomerania and previous member of the 'Totenkopf'- Re-

Murdered Jews at Pinsk

iterstandarte, were active in the area between Brest and Gomel. The first executions performed by this unit took place in Czuzewicze, and the bloody trail would run its course through Kamién, Koszyrski, Drozyn, and Janów. The bloodbath reached its apex at the commercial town of Pinsk, with 40.000 inhabitants, after at Janów 1.000 Jews had been murdered. Pinsk once again confirmed how different SS-organizations merged with regards to the Holocaust. In addition to the Waffen-SS, a unit under the command of SS-Hauptsturmführer was active here: the Sicherheitspolizei. Similar to other countries, a Jewish council was established in Pinsk which aided the

North of Pinsk, August 1941

Captured Soviet-soldiers

identification of Jews in the city. As a result mass murder could be executed more efficiently.

The Jews at Pinsk were gathered at the building of the secret military security service of the Soviet Union – NKWD – and transported to fields just outside the city. In a short amount of time more than 6.000 Jews were executed. On their way, approximately 100 Jews tried to escape, however, the Waffen-SS and their horses caught up to almost all of them. As with other executions, these murders were immediately reported to Von dem Bach-Zelewski who had come to visit Magill. Photographs of these death fields that still exist, depict chaotic surroundings. The bodies were scattered over a large surface. The killing machine of the SS hadn't yet evolved into the cold-blooded troops which were later known as the SS in the KZ's and the Einsatzgruppen. As the units of the Kommandostab finally put Pinsk behind them, 9.000 civilians had been executed. In the report a 'military spin' had been given to the performances. A member of the militia had supposedly been shot after which, as a retaliation, the Jews had to be murdered.

However, Pinsk wasn't the only town where tremendous things took place, which became evident during the regiments' continuous march towards Luninec where 1312 Jews were executed. At Davyd-Haradok a new massacre followed. Once again people witnessed the remarkable cooperation with the local population. While the SS shot the masculine population first, the non-Jewish citizens chased the Jewish women and kids out of the city on August 10. Several women were beaten to death while being chased out. The gathered Jewish community was searched and plundered at a bridge which led them out of town. Some men who had hid themselves between the women, were thrown into the river and drowned by the citizens. The Waffen-SS merely watched during these events. After the killing spree had come to an end, Magill reported that no fights had taken place. The tragedy at Davyd-Haradok had simply been murder. When Magill had completed his actions at the Pripyat swamps, approximately 14.000 Jews had been executed.

Massacres between Rowno and Shitomir

The operations of the Waffen-SS' infantry within the Kommandostab were, according to the 7.000 soldiers of the 1st SS-Brigade (mot.), no better. Inside the area of the HSSPF Friedrich Jeckeln at the Ukraine, rough-

The march of the SS-brigade

ly between Równo and Zhytomyr, troops were active. The end of July had been the date of commencement, and similar to other operations, cooperation with other units in addition to the Wehrmacht was immediate. The Wehrmacht operated under the command of general Karl Jerome Christian Georg Kurt von Roques, an officer from Frankfurt am Main who had made a name for himself at the conquered areas as a commander with brutal policies. His performances would lead to a twenty-year prison sentence after the war. He was the commander of the 142nd infantry division as well. Through Starokostiantyniv, where Jews had been living since the 16th century, the Waffen-SS infantry kept moving via Czetyrboki and Ostrog (August 4), leaving thousands of victims behind them. The Jewish community in Starokostiantyniv existed of approximately 5.000 inhabitants. What was interesting here is, as Cüppers mentioned, that during the murders at Ostrog, SS-Obersturnführer Otto Storch (Commander of the 9th company) asked his men if they wanted to participate. Ten to fifteen men dropped out after that. Some Waffen-SS soldiers thus found it difficult to take part in the murders. However, this did not affect the fate of the Jews: they were still murdered.

The *1st SS-Brigade's* (mot.) Common Front Work at Korosten

At the backdrop of the 6th German army (later known as the Stalingrad army) at the 1st SS- Brigade (mot.) it also came to fights against common Soviet troops. Here the Waffen-SS' infantrymen did their 'regular' military job, similar to other SS-troops which were stationed at the front. The losses ran up considerably during these fights. At Korosten the brigade met approximately 800 Red Army soldiers, who had gotten behind German lines and tried to break through. The brigade lost about 90 men to injuries and death during the confrontation. Units of the regular German forces were called for help. The deployment of Kommandostab troops was praised by the regular army, who rendered them with compliments and honor.

The previous argument shows how the Kommandostab belonged to the Waffen-SS. However, they were different from other Waffen-SS units who stood at the

DER KOMMANDIERENDE GENERAL
DER SICHERUNGSTRUPPEN UND BEFEHLSHABER IM HEERESGEBIET MITTE

AUSZUG FÜR DIE
⚡⚡ KAVALLERIE BRIGADE
FEGELEIN

24.7.1941 – 11.8.1941	Vernichtung eines russ. Kavallerie-Korps u. der 121. russ. Schützen-Division im Raum Sluzk–Bobruisk.
12.8.1941 – 1.10.1941	Kämpfe gegen versprengte Feindgruppen – Partisanen aus den Schlachten um Smolensk.
2.10.1941 – 9.12.1941	Kämpfe gegen versprengte Feindgruppen – Partisanen aus der Doppelschlacht Wjasma – Brjansk.

DER KOMMANDIERENDE GENERAL

v. Schenckendorff

GENERAL DER INFANTERIE

Wilno ⚡⚡

Praise to the Fegelein Brigade

front, while still being available for the HSSPF's bloody operations at the occupied Russian territories. Here the units operated independently, or in cooperation with other units, such as the Einsatzgruppen, the Ordnungspolizei and even the regular army, although they were only used in case of military necessity. However, also within the Kommandostab the tasks and operations weren't unambiguous. The 2nd SS infantry Brigade (mot.), who operated at the northern part (Baltic States) of the front was so absorbed with the front tasks and ant-partisan missions, that they weren't part of the large-scale massacres, which were quite common to the other units of the Kommandostab Reichsführer-SS. This also tied in to the fact that the unit existed of Dutch and Flemish volunteers of the Waffen-SS (primarily known as the 'legion').

The deployment and the administrative division of these units (the Waffen-SS, 'Diet's or 'German') were part of sensitive debate, during which the SS-Hauptamt and Himmler had to consider the sentiments at home. However, looking back we can conclude that it had been a close call or the Flemish and Dutch Waffen-SS had served with one of the most murderous formations at the eastern front. The fact remained that their brigade was at least on an administrative scale part of the killing machine. For the Flemish the war took place as a

'Kleinkrieg' around Andrianova and Tarassowa, and for the Dutch units it took place around Selo Gora and other small towns at the Wolchow-front.

'Difficult but Necessary'

After the days of August the deployment of the Kommandostab continued. Historically significant here is the visit made by Himmler, accompanied by his SS-confidants Karl Wolff and Han-Adolf Prützmann, to Lachow-

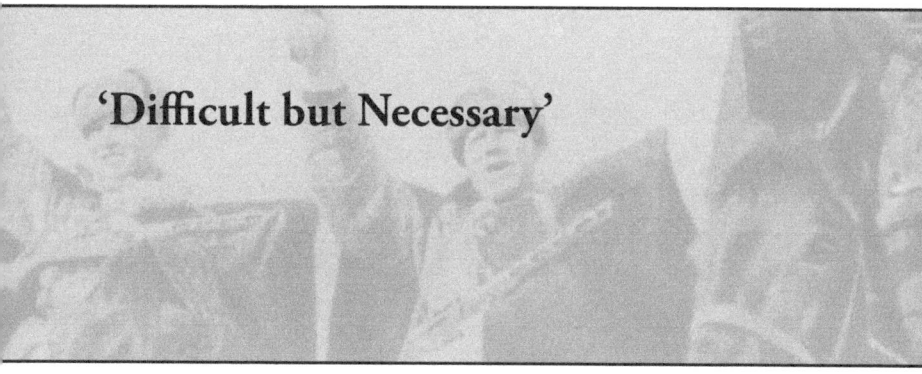
A purge operation

Faithful horses in an inhumane war

Von der Kühnheit.

Diese edle Schwungkraft, mit der die menschliche Seele sich über die drohendsten Gefahren erhebt, ist im Kriege auch als ein eigenes wirksames Prinzip, das heißt als Kraftquelle zu betrachten.

Sie ist vom Troßknecht und Tambour bis zum Feldherrn hinauf die edelste Tugend, der rechte Stahl, welcher der Waffe ihre Schärfe und ihren Glanz gibt. Aber den Erfolg des Kalküls mit Raum, Zeit und Größe hinaus müssen ihr noch gewisse Prozente zugestanden werden, die sie jedesmal, wo sie sich überlegen zeigt, aus der Schwäche der anderen zieht. Sie ist also eine wahrhaft schöpferische Kraft.

Je höher wir unter den Führern hinaufsteigen, je notwendiger wird es, daß der Kühnheit ein überlegener Geist zur Seite trete, daß sie nicht zwecklos, nicht ein blinder Stoß der Leidenschaft sei.

Mit einem Heer, das von einem kühnen Volk ausgegangen und in welchem der Geist der Kühnheit immer genährt worden ist, lassen sich andere Dinge unternehmen als mit einem, das dieser kriegerischen Tüchtigkeit entfremdet ist.

Eine durch vorherrschenden Geist geleitete Kühnheit ist der Stempel des Helden.

So glauben wir denn, daß ohne Kühnheit kein ausgezeichneter Feldherr zu denken ist, daß ein solcher nie aus einem Menschen werden kann, dem diese Kraft des Gemüts nicht angeboren ist.

Je größer diese Kraft noch ist, um so stärker ist der Flügelschlag des Genies, um so höher der Flug.

Das Wagnis wird immer größer, aber das Ziel wächst mit ihm.

Aus Clausewitz „Vom Kriege".

Der SS Kavallerie Brigade Fegelein

als Anerkennung für ihren erfolgreichen Einsatz bei den Winterkämpfen der 9. Armee im Raume um Olenin und bei Rshew

A.H.Qu., den 31. Mai 1942

Generaloberst und Oberbefehlshaber der 9. Armee

SS-Brigadeführer Hermann Fegelein

SS-Obergruppenführer Jüttner

SS-Oberführer Fegelein and SS-Brigadeführer Bittrich

icze where he visited units of the Waffen-SS cavalry. At Lachowicze, Himmler would have stated that people 'did not want to repeat the mistakes which had been made in Poland'. Here he aimed at the fact that the Jews were locked up in ghetto's first. Now they were murdered immediately. On August 14, after a visit to Minsk, Himmler witnessed a mass-execution of approximately a hundred men and women, after which he delivered a speech, in which he stated the task to be difficult but necessary. On August 16, Himmler flew back to Führer headquarters at Rastenburg, East Prussia, to personally inform Hitler of the progress that had been made.

Minsk 1941

Karl Wolff

Compromising

The deployment of the Kommandostab Reichsführer-SS in Russia showed how compromising operation 'Barbarossa' was. Massacres were part of everyday life. The perpetrators, however, were not only part of the Einsatz-

A drawing made by a Waffen-SS soldier:
'The Soviets used the church as a stable'

gruppen and the SS and SD. Local militias, police-units and the Waffen-SS took part in these operations. After the war, prominent Waffen-SS officers such as Paul Hausser and Felix Steiner, stated to emphasize that the Waffen-SS were primarily simple front soldiers. This was true for most of the divisions. However war crimes still occurred, for instance at the 'Dirlewanger' division who went on a rampage at Warsaw in 1944 and at former anti-partisan missions. However, within the Kommandostab the most large-scale violations of the martial law took place, and the performances of the brigades were known as war crimes and genocide.

The entire Third Reich distinguished itself with countless authoritative sources who were competing against each other. It was in that sense almost impossible to 'keep your hands clean', if one could even speak of such a thing, considering the fact that the attack on the Soviet-Union was in itself an act of aggression. The veil, covering the role of the Waffen-SS during this war of destruction, is to certain extent still visible today. Quite recently a reissue of, during the war, published writings of the SS-Kavallerie im Osten appeared at publishing house Arndt. In this 'frische' photo album the Waffen-SS soldiers and commander Fegelen, were literally referred to as boy scouts, and only shows photographic material of the brigade. The only battle mentioned, was the battle against the partisans. Mass executions were not spoken off. Also, in the introduction of this work, the actual performances of the brigade are missing. As a result, old myths are kept alive.

Questioning a Russian partisan

Paul Hausser

Rückwärtige Heeresgebietskommando – *a Forgotten Chapter*

The war crimes committed by the Kommandostab originated from Himmler's need for retribution to make his HSSPF at the occupied areas more powerful in comparison to the army. This, however, did not mean that

Roads were scarce in the area where the SS Cavalry Brigade was deployed

only the HSSPG, the brigades and the Einsatzgruppen had blood on their hands. Until now little attention has been paid to the role of the army itself, and especially the rückwärtiges Heeresgebietskommando; thus the military governance at the areas lying behind the front, which fell under the jurisdiction of the army (beside overlaps). In any case, it wouldn't be out of place if we continued to highlight the role of the Einsatzgruppen, especially since the 'Holocaust of bullets' has always been overshadowed by the history of the camps. However, recently a number of significant studies has appeared, including work by Ronald Headland, Ralf Ogorreck, Zvi Gitelman, Michel Moracchini and biographies concerning the perpetrators (Karl Jäger and Friedrich Jeckeln) written by Wolfram Wette and Bernard Kiekenap. Because of their work we leave this part of history as it is.

The fact that the army wasn't disconnected from Nazi-ideology became evident during the first meetings concerning 'Barbarossa', shortly after the summer campaign of 1940 against France. Chief of general staff Franz Halder stated in his journals, after a meeting with Hitler and the generals, that a war would commence 'between two ideologies', and that a 'devastating judgment call had been made concerning Bolshevism' which Hitler emphasized as 'criminal'. 'Communism was not an ally', he believed, 'and would never be one'. From his notes it became evident that Halder intended to completely get rid of communism, as it was not the intention to 'meet the communist enemy again in 30 years'. 'We should not fight to conserve our enemy', he stated, after which he determined his goals: 'the destruction of the commissioners and the communist intellectuals'. In that sense the war against Russia was a war of destruction on its own. It was even somewhat comparable to the campaign against Poland where people dealt with the Polish intelligentsia (the murder of professors) and the religious elite. The Soviets had taken care of the military elite with massive killing sprees, which became evident in the woods of Katyn, close to Smolensk. During this campaign approximately 22.000 Polish inhabitants were slaughtered.

It is remarkable to take note of the fact that not one of Hitler's generals protested against his destructive plans. Historian Jörn Hasenclever stated that no-one, on that infamous day of consultation of which Halder spoke, dared to go against Hitler's wishes. Hitler himself, did not have a lot of confidence in the 'noble generals' , even despite the lack of protest of the army. To his confidants, Alfred Jodl an Wilhelm Keitel, he emphasized that the imminent war 'would not merely be a war of arms'. The enemy state had to be 'completely obliterated'. The task of the army Hitler wanted to keep as small as possible, because they weren't the most sound vehicle to use during the war of destruction. Hitler desired to transform the military governance into a civil service, the so-called Reichskommissariaten where the permission of the politics mattered most, as soon as possible. Nevertheless, the commanders in the 'rückwärtse' areas (Korpsrückwärts-Korück and Befelshaberrückwärts-Berück) played their negative part.

The marching route of the 6th Pz. Div.

Max von Schenckendorff, Karl von Roques, Franz von Roques, and Erich Friderici

The names of these commanders are relatively unknown. Erroneously, as they were key figures during crucial moments of the campaign – and the Holocaust of bullets -, especially in terms of preparation work: the isolation and stigmatization of the Jews. There was additionally the cooperation with the death squads. The commanders it concerned were Max von Schenckendorff, Karl von Roques, Franz von Roques, and Erich Friderici.

Max von Schenckendorff was born on February 24, 1975 at Prenzlau and came from an ancient noble family that dated back to the thirteenth century. The so-called 'Schenckenländchen' at Berlin, was named after his family. He had experience as a fighter during the First World War, where he had served in the 64th infantry regiment. During the same war he also got an understanding of repressive measures against civilians. At the time he spoke of 'draconian measures', measures he defended as well, as people 'had to protect their men'. Here it concerned the Freischärlern' (or armed citizens), in Belgium, at a place called Bolland in August 1914, where, according to the Germans, the citizens turned on the soldiers. 'My heart skipped a beat', he stated, after the Germans had taken hostages, among who a mayor and the priest of a local town. However, Von Schenckendorff proved himself to be a hardliner and a determined soldier who was keen on taking on Paris. After some health issues (he suffered of migraine) he ended up in the 'etappe' (a logistical department). Here he was stationed at the Rekrutendepot of the 3rd Army corps.

At the Rekrutendepot he got acquainted with the area behind the front, the population, the administrative tasks that came with the job, and the danger of espionage and treason. The Rekrutendepot provided a realistic education for its recruits. Later on, Von Schenckendorff was additionally deployed east at – the 'by god abandoned Serbia' – after which he went to Belgium, Verdun, Saarburg (at Trier) and the battle for Champagne. He hadn't served at the front for quite some time. As son of a general he had escaped the horrors at the front during the First World War.

Later on in his life he was discovered by Erich Ludendorff, Paul von Hindenburg's right hand man, as

Erich Friderici

tactician and drill sergeant of officers and men. Von Schenckendorff soon became more important because of his educational talents, and as a result acknowledged as such by Ludendorff who, as 'Viceroy of Kowno' during his deployment at Oberost had done more work than was expected of him at the front. It was for a reason that people began to talk of 'Diktatur Ludendorff', because the OHL was also concerned with economics and propaganda. At the time Von Schenckendorff was related to the OHL, and deployed at the troops' educational unit called Arys. In addition, he made sure that the German infantry divisions were ready for the western front, after they had returned from the collapse of czarist Russia.

On an ideological scale the November-defeat had a major impact on Von Schenckendorff. He believed the peace of Versailles to be a 'disgrace' and deemed German politics as a 'deed of madness'. After the war Von Schenckendorff became a part of an army of 100.000 men and found himself in the right-conservative wing, filled with contacts of ex-combatant organizations who were affiliated with the Freikorpsen. He believed the 'Ertüchtigung' of the German youth to be his main assignment.

Karl von Roques was born on May 7, 1880 in Frankfurt am Main, and came from a noble family, where people were mostly active in the 'Beamtenum'. In the nineteenth century Von Roques' first sons served in das Militär. In 1912, Von Roques served in the 'Grossen Generalstab' and entered the First World War with the VIII. Reserve corps, which was a part of the 4th army. He became an experienced fighter at the 8th Reserve-division and the 215th Infantry division and fought at the Maas, Marne and at Champagne. He earned the EK-II and EK-I and was thus an experienced soldier. After the war he continued his work for the Ministry of Defense and served at the 1st Inf. Div for a short period of time. After a while he returned to civil life and worked at the Reichsluftschutzbund. He complained about the fact that he had not received a signed photograph of Hitler upon his departure, which said something about his political attitude. At the Bund he worked alongside Herman Göring, and returned to the army as General of the Flakartillerie (Air defense) where his administrative experience served him well as Befehlshaber Rückwärts.

Franz von Roques – not related to Karl von Roques – came from a bourgeois family and was born on September 1, 1877 at Treysau, Hessen. He served at many positions during the First World war. For instance, he was battalion commander, served the staff of the III. Bayern army corps, and later on, in 1917 served at the X. Army corps. The November-defeat was met with deep disappointment in the politics. He remained true

Max von Schenckendorf

to the military apparatus, primarily at his home unit, the 81st regiment. Afterwards staff functions at the Nachrichten - department at the Ministry of Defense followed, and duties at the General Kommando IX. He ended the France-campaign in May with his presence, when the French general surrendered at Compiègne, in the train compartment where the defeat of 1918 had been signed.

Erich Friderici was born on December 21, 1885 in Obersilezie at Pless. From 1904 he had served in the German army as Fahnenjunker (candidate-officer) and went to war with a Maschinengewehrkompanie in September 1914. Via his service at the 63rd Inf. Brigade he became staf-officer, where he saw the 'Michael'-offensive, the doubted German spring offensives of 1918, up close. After the war, Friderici remained active in military service, amongst the 4th division and Wehrkreis IV (military district) where he aided the reconstruction of the army. In October 1938 he became commander of the 17th Inf. Div. He gained administrative and political experience as a military attaché at Budapest. These experiences served him well when he was deployed in the Wehrkreis Böhmen und Mähren, where he drew up a report concerning 'Das Tsechechische Problem'. Here Friderici showed he did not only aspire military goals. He was also concerned with the defeat of the Czech resistance.

On march 15,1941 Max von Schenckendorff, Franz von Roques, Karl von Roques, and later on Friderici were appointed commanders of the Rückwärtiges Heeresgebietskommando. These military districts were divided in numbers, however, these numbers corresponded with the 'division' of Russia during operation 'Barbarossa' in north, middle, and south:

- rückwärtiges Heeresgebietskommando 101 (Nord).
- rückwärtiges Heeresgebietskommando 102 (Mitte).
- rückwärtiges Heeresgebietskommando 103 (Süd).

Immediately after the raid they were deployed. An aspect of their job was very visible, such as the operations of the Sicherungsdivisionen against partisans; other duties were less visible, the Meldewesen which fell under their command, for instance. Historian Hasenclever calculated that the Heeresgruppe Süd alone sent approximately 1200 to 1500 messages a day. During the first six months of 1942 alone, 5089 Geheimsachen (secret matters) were sent, messages which were thus considered extremely significant. The Militärverwaltung turned out to be a tremendous endeavor. It, was, however, comprised of more than the Sicherungsdivisionen. A lot of personnel was involved, and also the work troops of 'Organsation Todt', the Reichsarbeitsdienst, co-workers of the Reichsban (railroads) and the Wirtschaftsverwaltung (WiStab Ost) were involved. The entire complex, only within the Heeresgruppe Mitte, in the end, was comprised of approximately 400.000 soldiers.

Organisation Todt, paving the roads in Russia

The Unknown Reich

German Reichsbahn in Russia

Sicherungsdivisionen

The Sicherungsdivisionen, units which were never really given much attention in history, were fighting against the Soviet-partisans. At first it concerned three divisions per Heeresgebiet:

At the marching route

207de Sicherungsdivision (general Tiedemann)
- Heeresgebiet Nord
281ste Sicherungsdivision (general Bayer)
- Heeresgebiet Nord
285ste Sicherungsdivision (general Von Poltho)
- Heeresgebiet Nord
221ste Sicherungsdivision (general Pflugbeil)
- Heeresgebiet Mitte
286ste Sicherungsdivision (general Müller)
- Heeresgebiet Mitte
403de Sicherungsdivision (general Von Ditfurth)
- Heeresgenbiet Mitte
213de Sicherungsdivision (general de l'Homme de Courbiere)
 - Heeresgebiet Süd
444de Sicherungsdivision (general Russwurm)
- Heeresgebiet Süd
454de Sicherungsdivision (general Krantz)
- Heeresgebiet Süd

These divisions faced a difficult task. Their equipment was moderate, and existed primarily of stolen Czech and Belgian weapons, and the number of men, usually between the 7000 and 9000 per division, was significantly smaller compared to normal infantry divisions. In addition, they had few trucks at their disposal and the units were divided over the different Feldkommandanturen and the Ortskommandanturen, of which the most famous were Lviv, Lutsk, Tarnopol, Vilnius, Bialowieza, Daugavpils, Riga and Minsk. A difficult 'Kleinkrieg' commenced against Russian partisans, where thousands of partisans and soldiers of the Sicherungsdivisionen lost their lives. During these fights, the divisions were also deployed against units of the Red Army, Soviet air landing operations, pilots from shot down airplanes, and

Additional success to the 'Blitzkrieg'

air strikes. The most important task was reserved for the defense units of the significant provisioning nodes. The force of attack, however, was restricted and people often referred to defensive attacks. The officers belonged to second classes and were often of age. Hasenclever calculated that 88 officers were sent home shortly after the commencement of operation 'Barbarossa' as they were deemed unfit. The war against the Partisans developed into an ugly conflict. However, this was a known fact and basically the nature of operation Barbarossa, which was based on terror and destruction. Nevertheless, the commander of the 213th Sicherungsdivision was concerned about the fact that parts of his troops were too indifferent and care-free opposite the local population; which could potentially be a threat. On the other hand, the war led to chaotic situations because of the cruelties committed by both sides. The commander of the 221st Sicherungsdivision, warned for random German acts of revenge, after the discovery of murdered German soldiers.

Bielsk and Vilnius – the Cooperation between Einsatzgruppen and Sicherungsdivisionen

The measures taken against the partisans, for instance a grand-scale operation at von Scheckendorffs area, where approximately 2000 men were arrested, harmonized with anti-Jewish operations. Military officers actively aided

An injured Soviet soldier and Waffen-SS troops

the preparations made by the Einsatzgruppen, by dispossessing, stigmatizing, and gathering the Jews. They were additionally asked to aid during the war violence repairs. People forced the Jews to pay themselves for their own work. The diligence with which people operated within the Heeresgruppe Nord, became evident at the 504th infantry regiment of the 291st division (not a Sicherungsdivision). Ten days before the official command came through to arrest the Jews and mark them with stars, the regiment had already begun. The Ortskommandant of Bielsk, who was under the command of Berück/Korück, established a Jew Council. At Bielsk all events took place in cooperation with the Einszatsgruppen who massacred the population. In Vilnius, the same occurred. Not all German authoritative sources supported the anti-Semitism. Especially economic units, such as the Wirtschaftsinspektion Süd, emphasized that the exclusion of all Jews from social life could have negative consequences. Among them were many experts and craftsmen who wanted to work. As a result, the Wirtschaftsinspektion Süd suggested to leave the exclusion and the definitive Jew politics to the Reichskommissare, who, if the fighting was over, would have the final say.

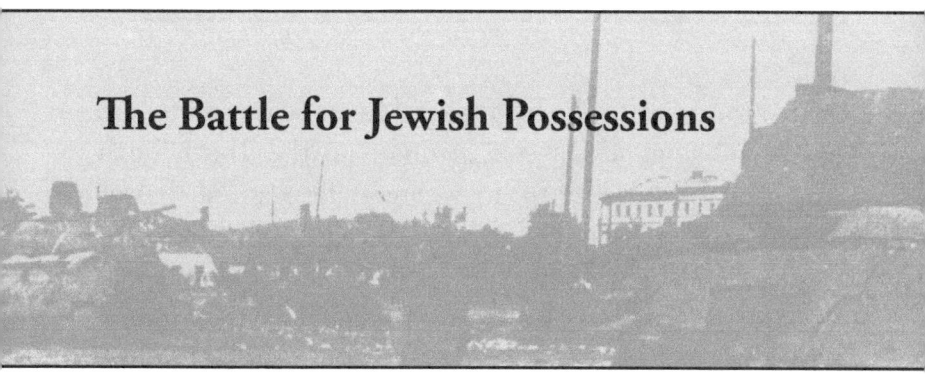

The Battle for Jewish Possessions

Remarkable was the discussion concerning Jewish possessions – to who did they belong? Von Schenckendorff stated on July 8,1941 that this had become a current issue because Korück, in addition to Sipo and the SD

Hotel *Molochow*, Smolensk

tried to proclaim the belongings. Again, clear guidelines were missing, which was common to the Third Reich as it enabled Hitler to do whatever he wanted. It was the Wirtschaftsstab Ost, who, in the end, gained the upper hand. This also brought forward the double agenda, people wanted to spare the Jews – for their own industrial gain – however, they also did not want to lose the possessions of the murdered Jews. The attitude towards the Jews, after the 'victory' of the 'inheritance', became more severe. According to the Wirstschaftsstab Ost, the Jews had suddenly become 'the propagandists of the Soviet-system' and 'agitators'. People pleaded to place the Soviet Jews in ghetto's and concentration camps.

Korück's first big 'test', with regards to the Jews, was to Von Schenckendorff the city of Minsk, a city with 140.000 inhabitants and a large Jewish population. Von Schenckendorff gave the command to round up the Jews in a ghetto. In addition, the Jews were used for city repairs, were forced to give up their homes to other citizens, and strictly rationed. A Jewish council and several Jewish laws established. The ghetto of Minsk was the first in a long line of ghetto's that were established because of military management: Bialystok, Baranovichi, Vitebsk and Smolensk followed as well. The Einsatzkommando 2 praised the cooperation with the military management, which turned out to be 'very successful'.

However, the position of the military management remained ambivalent. Jörg Hasenclever, for instance, states that a commander such as Von Schenckendorff wasn't particularly anti-Jewish as he had commented on the execution of Jews is Ostrow-Mazowiecka (he questioned the legal justification). However, under his command the 221st Sicherungsdivision cooperated with the 309th Polizeibataillon which was responsible for burning down the synagogue of Bialystok where 800 people died. In all, at least – the numbers originate from Germans documents – 500.000 people were murdered in the areas behind the Soviet fronts.

The real numbers were significantly higher. The Jews murdered by the Romanians, for instance, were not mentioned in the Ereignissmeldungen of the Einsatzgruppen. One estimates that in October 1941 approximately 600.000 Jews were killed by the Romanians in the city of Odessa. This number wasn't a part of the 91.278 murders reported by the Einsatzgruppe D (who operated in the South). Historian Ronald Headland concludes in his book *Message of Murder,* that the total amount of victims should be estimated at about 1.152.731 people. Most of these murders were accounted to the Einsatzgruppen A, B, C, and D, immediately followed by the efforts made by the units of the HSSPF, the brigades and police.

Famine

Little has been published about the famine in Russia, especially during 'Barbarossa'. Most stories concerning this topic are about the Holodomor in the Ukraine in the thirties, the terrible 900-days siege of Leningrad, the

Smolensk after heavy street fights

scarcity at the 6th army at Stalingrad, and the famine in the prison camps. Less known is the famine which eventually even led to cannibalism at the closed off Soviet armies close to the river the Volchov, at the northern side of the eastern front. However, especially the civilian population was systematically hungry in the occupied German territories.

Here it was once again the result of competition between several departments. It was simply not taken care of properly. Soon the German forces uncovered that the European horse did not function well on the robust Russian land. As a result Russian horses were stolen. Numbers indicate that in the territory of the Heeresgruppe Nord approximately 60.000 horses were confiscated. Soviet agriculture, however, greatly depended on the use of horses and the consequences were insurmountable.

Soviet civilians at Smolensk, a private photograph taken by a German soldier

Between Apathy and Revolt

The army additionally struggled with the troops' provisioning and partly lived off the lands, which put a large strain on the population. The hunger was first noticeable in the larger cities. When it struck, 12.000 citizens left

Defeated anti-aircraft guns, Smolensk 1941

the city of Smolensk in a short amount of time, while tens of thousands of people had already left the city before the arrival of the Germans. As a result, the cities of occupied Russia looked abandoned and had turned into ghost towns.

Approximately 800.000 citizens were on the move in 1941 and 1942 as a direct result of the famine. The Germans were afraid of the term 'famine' as everyone feared the consequences. Von Schenckendorff and Franz von Roques had warned about the consequences that would follow the rigid exploitation of the civilian population. It would push the citizens back into the arms

The 6th Pz. Div. at a parade in Krefeld, on the eve of the Russia-campaign. The division had Czech tanks at its disposal

Anton Groder †

Gedenket im Gebete
des Soldaten
Anton Groder
Moisohn in Kals

der am 31. Juli 1941 im Alter von 27 Jahren
an der russischen Front gefallen ist.

Herr, verleihe ihm die ewige Siegespalme!

Dein junges Leben, der Heimat gebracht,
ruht nun im Herrn; was Er gemacht,
ist wohlgetan; wir nehmen es an
und fragen still, was der Vater will.
Gib Frieden, Herr und ewige Ruh
Und führe uns alle der Heimat zu.

Mein Jesus, Barmherzigkeit!
(100 Tage Ablaß).

Süßes Herz meines Jesu, gib, daß ich
immer mehr dich lieb'!
(300 Tage Ablaß).

Süßes Herz Jesu, sei meine Liebe!
(300 Tage Ablaß).

Süßes Herz Maria, sei meine Rettung!
(300 Tage Ablaß).

An obituary. The infantry paid the price

of the Soviet-propaganda. Difficult as well, was the fact that the compensation received for working for the Germans was significantly reduced. Realistically speaking it wasn't beneficial anymore to work for the Germans as it didn't enable people to buy food on the black market. The population had its backs against the wall and were forced into the arms of the partisans. In November 1941, the German management decided to introduce food cards, with which people were able to deal with this problem. However, there was a fine line between apathy and revolt, between which the emaciated population was trapped. Several people looked for a way out by working in Germany. As a result, approximately 20.000 citizens left Stalino and headed west. According to Moscow, those people were collaborationists: however, in reality they were starving people who had their backs against the wall.

The streets of Smolensk

The Losses of Soviet-tanks and the Remarkable Resemblance of Losses between 1941 and 1945

On a military scale the war between Nazi-Germany and the Soviet-Union was unique in a negative sense. It was the biggest campaign ever. Speaking in numbers a lot of remarkable things can be said. It is generally known that

A heavy Russian tank

the losses of the Red Army at the beginning of the war were immense. This also applied to the armored defenses. It was estimated that the Red Army lost on average in 1941 (June up to December), about 3.723 tanks a month. What little people know is that the losses of the Soviet-Union in the glorious year of 1945 were almost the same. The average loss of tanks in 1945 was 3.186. This number was significantly higher than the average loss in 1942 (1.403 a month), in 1943 (1.958 a month), and 1944 (1.975 a month). These numbers show how the Red Army forcefully ended the war in 1945.

Pz.Rgt. 11 of the 6th Pz. Div. at Warsaw

A defeated heavy Russian tank, type T-28

Defeated Soviet-tanks at Roslawl

Their performance was the immediate result of the march to the west and Stalin's desire to reach across Germans borders as far as possible to strengthen his position during negotiations. However, it has to be taken into account that the losses of 1941 were more devastating. The Soviet production of tanks in 1941 was about 819 tanks a month (which was at the time a reasonable amount). However, approximately 2.940 tanks were lost each month as well. The production of tanks in 1945 came to 2.462 a month making the losses in comparison a bit less, although the loss of tanks would grow each month with 724 in 1945. In 1942 the most tanks were produced (656 tanks a month minus the losses).

Heavy Russian tanks (depicted is the Kv-2 tank) which surprised at Rossini

The Red Air Force – Astronomical Losses Throughout the War, However, the Industry was Spared

As the Germans invaded the Soviet-Union large parts of the Russian industry and raw materials threatened to fall into German hands. Hastily parts of the strategic industry were moved east. This was most successful for the

Soviet pilot at the 4th Ukrainian front. Throughout the war Soviet losses were astronomical

Russian pilot Ivan Tushev who was active above the Leningrad-front

Soviet pilot Alexander Jlubov. He died in 1944 along with thousands of other pilots

Russian aviation industry. Safeguarding this branch of the economy became top priority to the Kremlin. The evacuation was a remarkable accomplishment as it required massive logistical operations. In May 1941, on the eve of the attack, no less than 537.000 people worked in the industry. Because of evacuation and the rebuild this number would increase to 613.000 workers.

The evacuation, however, could not protect the Red Army from heavy blows during the early stages of the war. In the first six months of 1941, the Red Air force lost 17.900 airplanes. Some German pilots were praised

A defeated Red Army airplane

Me. 109

and became famous, Erich Hartman, for instance. He was nicknamed the 'black devil of the Ukraine' as he shot down hundreds of planes with the Jagdgeschwader 52. He became the most successful pilot during the war. Many of these planes had been destroyed on the ground during surprise attacks of Göring's Luftwaffe. The Soviet-losses were so great, Hermann Göring, chief of the Luftwaffe and Hitler's confidant, distrusted the reports. He immediately sent an inspection command into the field, after which he reported the losses to be even greater than primarily assumed. It took approximately an entire year before the Red Army recovered and the industry in Oral functioned once again.

Soviet-pilot Alexander Karpov, 37 victories

Russia's finest pilot, Ivan Kozhedub, 62 victories

Erich Hartmann, Germany's most successful fighter pilot

Fernschreibstelle — *Geheim*

Geheime Kommandosache

Fernschreiben

+ SSD LBKW NR. 02516 28/8 1255 =

AN OBERLEUTNANT ERICH HARTMANN STAFFELKAPITAEN 9./J.G. 52 –
MEIN LIEBER HARTMANN, MIT BEWUNDERUNG UND STOLZER FREUDE
BEGLUECKWUENSCHE ICH SIE ZU DER IHNEN VOM FUEHRER
VERLIEHENEN HOECHSTEN DEUTSCHEN TAPFERKEITSAUSZEICHNUNG.
IN EINEM SIEGESZUG OHNEGLEICHEN HABEN SIE DURCH
VORBILDLICHEN SCHNEID UND BEISPIELGEBENDE EINSATZFREUDIGKEIT
ALS ERSTER DEUTSCHER JAGDFLIEGER DIE EINZIGARTIGE ZAHL VON
301. ABSCHUESSEN ERREICHT. IHRE IN DEN BESTEN TUGENDEN
UNVERGAENGLICHEN DEUTSCHEN FLIEGERGEISTES WURZELNDEN
LEISTUNGEN SCHREIBEN DER GESCHICHTE UNSERER LUFTWAFFE NEUE
RUHMREICHE SEITEN. DAS DEUTSCHE VOLK ERBLICKT IN IHNEN
VOLL DANKBARKEIT EINEN SEINER KUEHNSTEN HELDEN. –
UNSERER JUGEND SIND SIE DURCH IHREN FANATISCHEN
KAMPFESWILLEN EIN LEUCHTENDES BEISPIEL UNBEZWINGBAREN
HELDENTUMS. MIT MEINEN GRUESSEN UND MEINER ANERKENNUNG FUER
IHRE UEBERRAGENDEN ERFOLGE VERBINDE ICH DEN WUNSCH, DASZ
IHNEN A[...] N
SEIN MOEGE. =

IHR GOERING, REICHSMARSCHALL DES GROSSDEUTSCHEN REICHES
UND OBERBEFEHLSHABER DER LUFTWAFFE. +

A congratulatory letter to Hartmann

The Beobachter (an air scout)

Junkers (ju) 87-'Stuka'

'Luftwaffe' soldiers under inspection

The Red Air Force – Astronomical Losses Throughout the War

Unknown and remarkable to these Red Air Force losses is the fact that - in comparison to the losses of tanks – they remained astronomically high throughout the war, so much that the losses of 1941 set a standard for the remainder of the war. An estimate of the Soviet aircraft losses between 1941-1945 was:

The pilot Erich Hartmann and his wife Ursula

1941: 17.900
1942: 12.000
1943: 22.000
1944: 30.000
1945: 18.000 (over the course of four months)

The Baltic fleet's airplanes

Luftwaffe-commander Göring. Depicted in the back is General Keitel

Stuka

Czech Tanks for the Wehrmacht

A lot can be said of the German army invading the Soviet-Union that has never ended up in history books. Approximately 25% of the 'Blitzkrieg's' tanks came from Czechoslovakia, because the Germans had captured its

35 (t) in Russia

Skoda- and CKD-factories. Early on the Czechs had developed a pretty ambitious program for its tanks which had commenced in 1933. In 1936 people desired to own about 1.000 tanks, among which they differentiated between cavalry tanks (light) and infantry tanks (heavy and middle class tanks). Via the MU-4, MUV-4 and the MUV-6 prototypes, they developed a 7-ton (exploration) tank with a 47mm canon. After some trial runs and several improvements made at the training area of Milovice, the tank was prepared for export. Through this strange twist of fate the vehicle was introduced to the Red Army – against who these tanks were heavily used by German armored troops. The shipment to Russia was cancelled because the sly Russians merely desired to buy one tank, after which Prague feared the rebuild of unlicensed copies. If this hadn't taken place, the Red Army could have fought off the Germans in 1941 with their own weapons. On the way back to Czechoslovakia, Romania quickly confiscated the new 7-ton tank to 'learn the secrets of the trade'. The tanks were thus in demand and exported to many countries. The Skoda-tanks were competitors of the British Vickers, the Polish 7 TP, the Italian 11/39 and 12/40, and the Russian T-26.

In March 1939 the Tanks were made available to the German army. The Pz.Rgt.11 was the first German

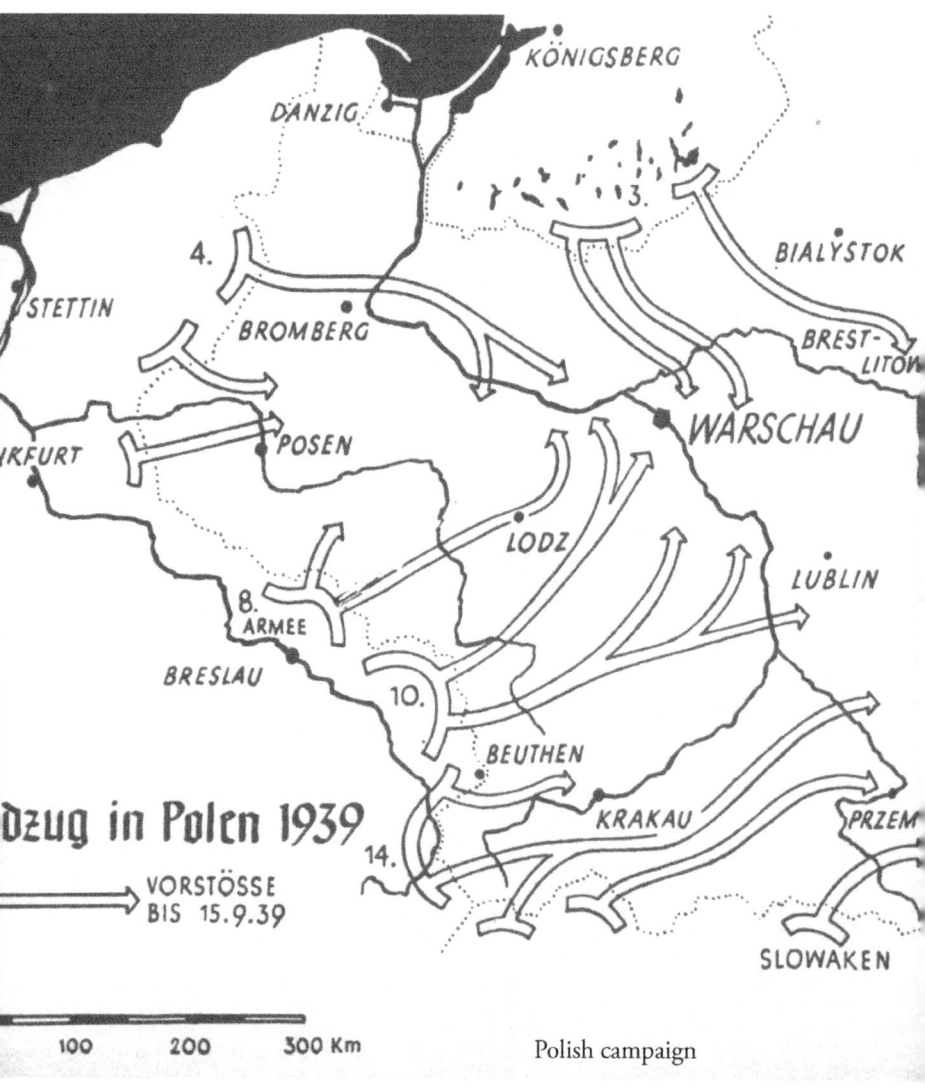

Polish campaign

unit who was equipped with the Skoda-tanks. At first people spoke of the Skoka Pz.III, however, the official name became PzKpfwg 35(t). 122 of these Panzerkampwagens were assigned to the Pz.Rgt 11. The German general staff had tested the Tanks from Pilsen and stated them to be 'useful'. The PzKpfw 38 (t). also turned out to be useful. In the summer of 1941, 763 of these tanks, produced in the Bömisch-Mährischen Maschinenfabrik of Prague, were made available to the German army. The tank had already proved its utility during the Poland-campaign, when these tanks, after a trial run at Neuhammer as part of the XIV Army corps (1. Leichte Division) of general Von Wietersheim, were deployed against Poland in 1939. This corps was part of the 10th army which, with 300.000 soldiers

Czech tanks serving the German army

was considered the strongest German force. Although some things went wrong, the unit operated successfully. In a reckless mood the 4th Kavallerieschützenregiment, under the command of Oberstleutnant Von Ravenstein, tried to conquer the Wartha-brigde. During a night raid the 5th Schwadron was deployed. However, the Polish were vigilant and met the Germans with deadly fire. Von Ravenstein's initiative had failed. Rittmeister Böcher was more successful at the bridge of Rychlocice, although it had partly been blown up. Although Polish soldiers put up a good fight, tanks of the 11th II./Pz.Rgt successfully placed the eastern bank under attack, after which the grenadiers could form a bridgehead.

38 (t.)

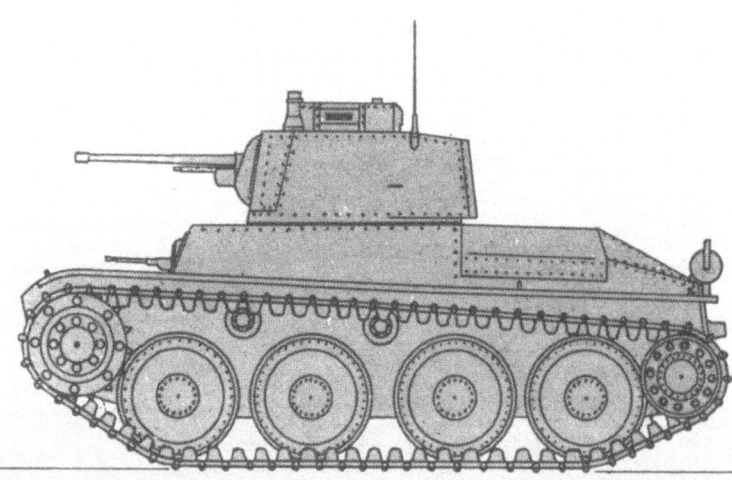

The Czech tanks operated perfectly, and many Polish units were surrounded between large rivers. The Polish retreat was chaotic and it was difficult for the Polish soldiers to make well-organized counter-attacks. The 'Blitzkrieg' was functioning. On September 11 a first encounter was made with Polish tank troops, which was properly dealt with, with the help of the Czech tanks of the 11th Pz.Rgt. Eight Polish tanks were confiscated. Afterwards fights at Studzianka-Rydswol erupted, after which 1.000 Polish soldiers were made prisoners of war. Next was the march towards Modlin, where at Lomna heavier fighting commenced. To give an impression of the losses: the 1st Leichte lost until September 13, 110 soldiers, counted 236 injured and 22 missing. At the 19th the division was deployed at purge operations in wooded areas surrounding Janówek, Buda, and Laski. The German high command had to make do, because this was in fact infantry work. A handful of tanks was lost as a result. However, as part of the encirclement ring which was drawn between Warschau and Modlin, it was

35 (t.)

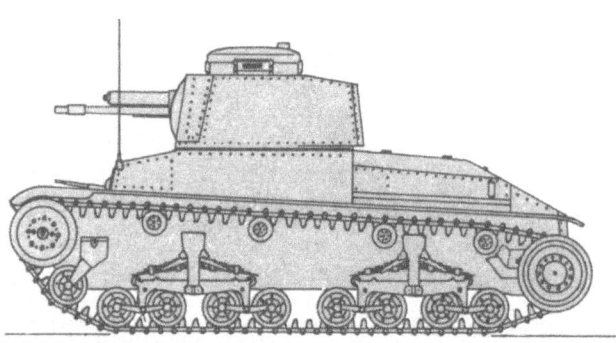

strategically defendable. The never ending support of the air force and especially the Stuka's (dive bombers) were essential during these fights.

A light weight Polish tank

Polish prisoners of war

The Battle of the Tanks at Rossieni

After the Poland-campaign, the France-campaign commenced where the 1st Leichte – later transformed into the 6th Pz. Div. – operated between Monthermé to Épinal, in order to march towards Leningrad in June

A staff meeting at the 6th Pz.Div

General Erich Hoeppner

1941 with the Russia-campaign, within the army group North. There the Czechoslovakian tank met its competitor. In the hills east of Rossieni and at the airport of Erzwilkas a new enemy stepped forward: the super heavy Soviet-tanks, the KwI and KwII. The 57th Pz. Aufklärungsabteilung met the 'monsters' first. The anti-tank canons of 1.46 and 1.97 inch did not stand a chance and were destroyed. Additionally the 11th Pz. Rgt tanks were unable to withstand the Kw's armor. According to Major Zollenkopf, battalion commander at the 114th Pz. Gren. Rgt., it never came to a Russian breakthrough because of bad cooperation between the Soviet-infantry and the armored weapons, otherwise the

A German anti-aircraft gun is deployed against tanks

future would have been bleak for the 6th Pz. Div. and the other units of the 56th Pz. Corps (Von Manstein), as part of the 4th Pz. Gruppe.

However, the 6th Pz. Div was the only German tank division who only used Czech tanks during the Russia-campaign. As a result, they were able to work with light bridges in the area of the 6th Pz.Div, enabling the division to operate fairly quickly. Also the maneuverability of the relatively light weight tanks was excellent and lent itself well for mobile tasks. However, at Rossieni it became evident that the soldiers who used Soviet-tanks found an enemy of considerable standards. The German tanks additionally struggled against the heavy Kw-tanks. They are fearless infantrymen, Leutnant Eckhardt, for instance, with a T-mine, and the heavy aviary artillery men of the 88th mm (Flakabteiling 21) and the 76th Pz. Art.Rgt. (Oberleutnant Bering), who, with immediate blows, ended the Soviet counterattacks. However, it was a close call and Generaloberst Erich Hoeppner of the 4th Pz. Gruppe, personally handed the EK-1 over to the soldiers who played a crucial part. Most of the Czech tanks met their maker at the gates of Moscow in the winter of 1941-1942, although on June 1, 1942, 167 tanks were still active in the German army. In May 1942 the 6th Pz. Div was transferred to Bretagne where they, at the training area of Coetquidan, were initiated to new tanks, especially PzKw III tanks and 1.97 and 2.95 inch canons. Later on during the war the division would switch to Pzkw IV tanks and the 'Panther'.

Soviet-losses were astronomical.
Depicted is a defeated T-26

The Unknown Reich

A semi-heavy German tank

'Marder' and 'Hetzer'

The German advantage would not be limited to the 35th (t) and the 38th (t) tanks. To fulfill the need for anti-tank weapons, a mobile artillery was developed. It concerned anti-tank artillery on tracks – Panzerjäger on Selbstfar-

Marder-III

hlafette (Sfl). The tested Czech tank proved to be useful as well. Here the Germans made use of the large number of Soviet anti-tank canons which were confiscated and installed on the Czech tanks. It concerned 3 inch canons (Pak: Panzerafwehrkanone 36) named Sd.Kfz. 139, which were later on renamed as 'Marder III', on Hitler's command and deployed. The tank fighter had 30 grenades at its disposal and gave refuge to the infantry against Soviet-tanks. The 'Marder III' was produced in the Böhmisch-Mährischen Maschinenfabrik at Prague, where the 38th (t) was also produced. In March 1943 an improved version was made, and in total about 800 'Marder III' were produced in total. The Jagdpanzer 38 'Hetzer' was also produced at Prague, in addition to several specialist armor vehicles: Bergepanzer (salvage tank), Flammenwerferpanzer and Flakpanzer (air defense tank), where the addition of the 38th (t) reminded one of its Czech origin. The factory in Pilsen also produced smaller armored vehicles during the war, the T15 and T25, for instance. Von Senger und Etterlin, at the time commander of among others the 17th Pz. Div. typified these armored vehicles as very good and especially also mobile, with a maximum speed of 37 miles an hour. All in all we can say that the 'Blitzkrieg' concept was greatly indebted to the Czech engineers, factories, and weapons. Von Senger and Etterlin had worked with Czech weapons during the liberation attempt of the 6th army in Stalingrad, during operation 'Wintergewitter' which, mostly because of a lack of troops – mainly infantry – eventually didn't succeed.

Flakpanzer

The Unknown Reich

Marder III

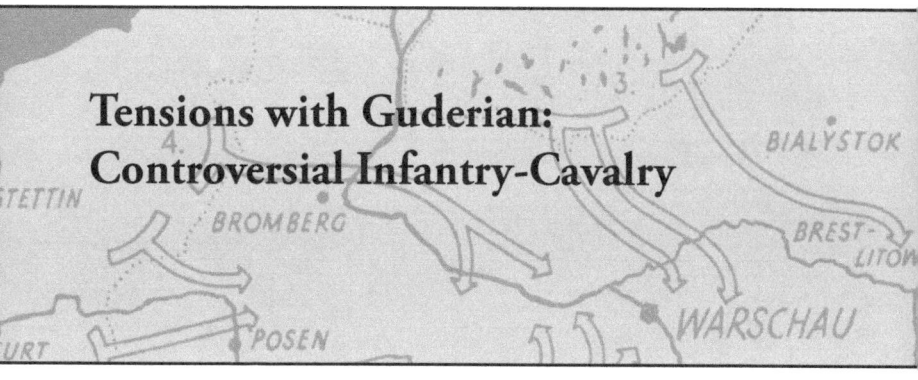

Tensions with Guderian: Controversial Infantry-Cavalry

To the outsider, the German army was a well-oiled machine that invaded the Soviet-Union. Less known are the tensions between the 'sand hares' of the infantry and the 'Gespenster'-soldiers of the tank divisions and motorized units. At the western front the armored troops were often held back to wait for the infantry, however, the petty depth of the front turned out to be in favor of the Germans. In the funnel-shaped width of the Russian surroundings the rate difference between the infantry and motorized units continued to haunt them. The result was often a tense relationship between the impatient tank officers and the infantry, where criticism went back and forth. In historiography most of the attention had gone out to the standpoints and positions of 'quickly moving troops', the memoires of tank specialist Heinz Guderian, for instance. However, it did not mean that his ideas and visions were correct. Typical, for instance, was the con-

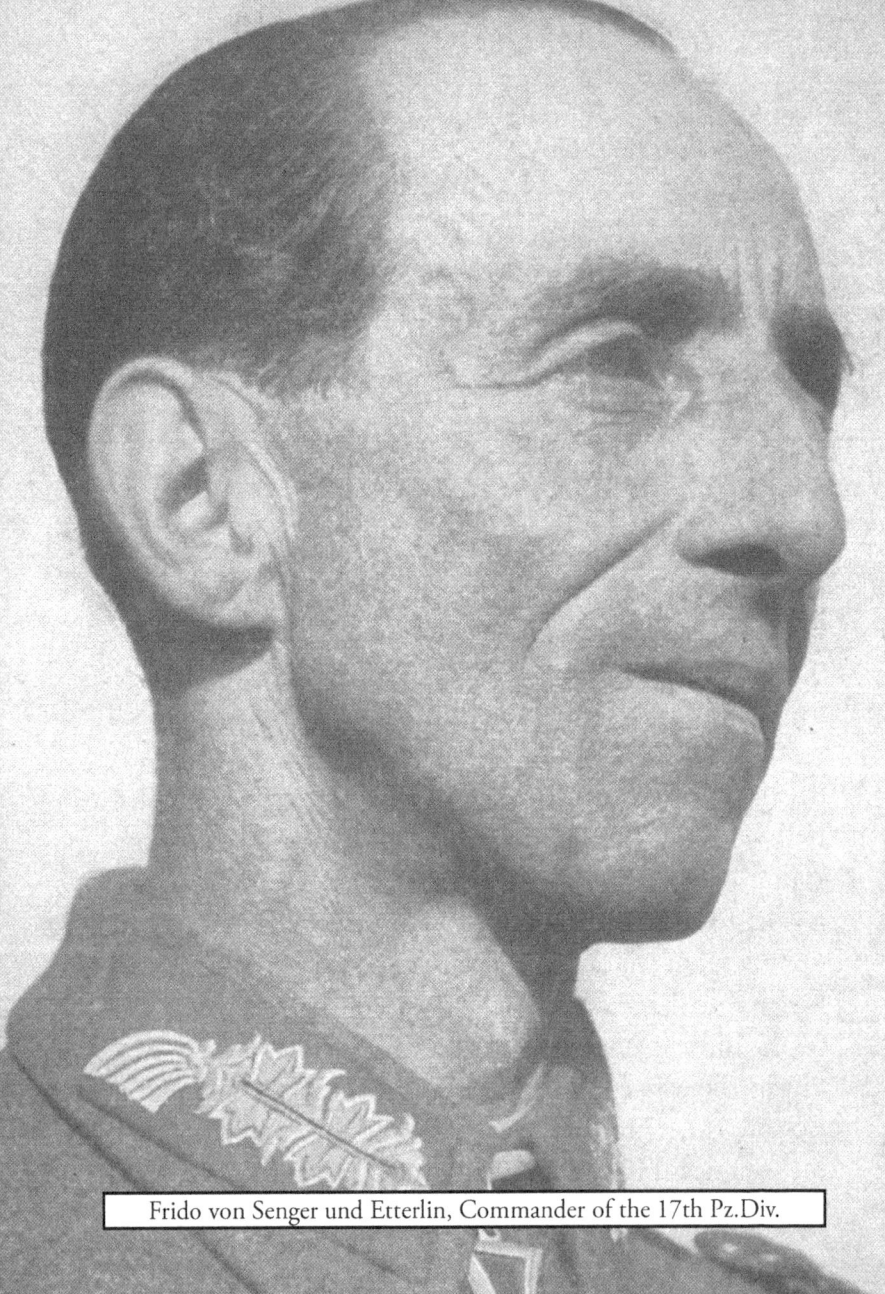
Frido von Senger und Etterlin, Commander of the 17th Pz.Div.

Heinz Guderian, 'He complained about the 'slow infantry'

Armored General Heinz Guderian in action

flict between the 137th Infantry division and Guderian's quickly moving troops in the summer of 1941. Guderians fast units, the Pz. Gruppe Guderian, operated in the area of the Heeresgruppe Mitte. The first fights in which these unites got involved were the battles at Bialystok, Minsk and especially Smolensk. The operations at Bialystok and Minsk belonged to the encirclement battles at the border. In his memoires Guderian wrote how the armored units established the encirclement, but wanted to withhold as little force as possible to enforce the encirclement and destroy the surrounding troops. The aim after all was faced forward. Afterwards an appeal had to be made to the undermentioned infantry-units. Here the 137th infantry division stepped forward. This division was one of the nameless faces at the front, but formed the bulk of the troops. The division was established in October 1941 in Austria. The commander was an experienced man, the 57-year old Generalleutnant Freidrich Bergmann, who at that time had served for 38 years and had already established the 27th ID. At the troops' training area called Döllersheim, the division was prepped for the front. Afterwards a training in Poland took place. The invasion of the Soviet-Union was the baptism of fire to the division.

The infantry paid a bloody price

The 137th Iinfantry Division

From its first day operation 'Barbarossa' took its toll. The Soviets turned out to be tough defenders, and also during the general retreat, groups remained in the villages and woods to offer resistance. In addition, the Red Army

Bridgehead Woronesh

General Bergmann, Commander of the 137th ID

was clever as it deployed snipers, and people did not shy away from unorthodox measures. For instance, in June a Soviet-sniper with a telescope rifle was captured wearing plain civilian clothing. The heat was almost unbearable and the condition of the roads miserable. The motorized German units got precedence on the few proper roads, the infantry was forced to march through the fields. Soldiers also got acquainted with Soviet-tank weapons. An infantry man wrote: 'Never in my entire life have I witnessed something this terrible. As common soldier one is simply powerless'. While the division was part of the encompassing units at the encirclement of many Soviet-divisions at Bialystok and Minsk, small 'Kessel'- battles took place between German and Russian battalions. At Bielsk it ended up to be a fight where the 137th ID killed 500 Russian soldiers and captured 150. Eighteen tanks were destroyed, because of the deployment of the 137th Artillery Regiment. It often turned out to be a close call, because the Red Army desperately tried to reach the east. The howitzers were often forced to shoot point blank into the crowds of breaching Russian troops.

Also during the marches towards Smolensk bitter fights took place. The Red Army had entrenched itself well and fought bravely. At Dubrovka and Borodino things got serious. A soldier of the 5th company of the 448th

Regiment spoke of a 'black day to the company'. He wrote: *'the Russians are firing at our advance route. It is eight o'clock in the morning, what a mortal fire. We are likely to attack. A terrible blow. The Russians do not know how to stop. We have to force them from their positions, from all bunkers people are shooting at us [..] we suffered many losses* (the names follow of 12 killed and 26 injured)'. However, after the so-called black day, the 137th division could boast about a victory. Big parts of the 18th and 73rd Russian infantry division were

The 137th ID's Russian prisoners of war at Wjasma

destroyed. The German losses added up to 500 killed and injured, of which most had fallen during the fights in the woods.

The battle for Wjasma, the artillery supports the 448th Inf.Rgt.

Borodino

The fights at Borodino were a breaking point in the discussion whether the tens of thousands of enclosed Red Army soldiers could break through to the east. The 137th ID was able to keep the frontlines closed, however, they

Czech tanks in Russia

paid a bloody price. During these fights the utmost was asked of the infantry and especially the artillery. It often occurred, for instance, that the artillery regiment was shooting point blank (with a flat range) at the breaching Russians, after which they were immediately forced to change directions to help six miles down the road, where they were needed most. The infantry was literally exhausted. At Zukowo the 449th regiment was forced to fight non-stop for seven hours against the Red Army. The fights were also very cruel. An artillery-department of the 137th regiment had been trampled by the Red Army, and prisoners of war were shot immediately by the Russians. Approximately 2.600 prisoners of war were counted and 50 artillery pieces were confiscated by the 137th ID. Historian Wilhelm Meyer-Detring stated that the appreciation for the division at Borodino was insufficient. After all, the results weren't only measured by the number of immediate prisoners, but also by the prevention of the breach. The success of the 137th ID was especially measured with the question when they would be connected to the tank units of Heinz Guderian and the 4th Pz. Army of Von Kluge, which focused its attention primarily on Smolensk and Jelnja. The fact that the 137th ID had been fighting for ten days against the remainder of the Soviet troops, was according to large operation maps which depicted the march, not important. General

Geyer felt the pressure of the tank troops and stated that his IX Army corps which belonged to the 137th ID, the 263rd ID, and the 292nd ID, 'should march onwards without looking after the neighbors, and advance east as a bolt of lightning. However, this was easier said than done, especially when considering the tough Red Army. In addition, when the armored troops stated they 'needed rest' and had to 'freshen up', the pressure increased. The reason for this necessary period of rest was that people were afraid they would lose their 'Schwung' during the attacks. Straight from the Borodino-fights the 137th ID was pushed forward to stand in for the 29th (mot.) division. To the infantry this was very disappointing. One had hoped to lean on the fire power and mobility through contact with the motorized troops. An officer of the 137th ID put is as such: 'We had suffered less losses, however, the road that lay behind us left us exhausted [..] now we were forced to take the defense upon ourselves, so others could rest. It was difficult. We also felt the need for rest and refreshments. However, everyone who thought on an operative scale, and not based on immediate interests, knew that our efforts were necessary in order to be quickly mobilized afterwards. That is why we sacrificed ourselves'. General Geyer stated: 'It was disappointing. The division had gone through some difficult times. Nevertheless it was self-evident that the 137th ID rushed to help out. The fact that we could stand in on July 24 at Smolensk was great'. At a Hotel in Smolensk called Molochow the division commander of the 137th ID was brought up to speed by Generalleutnant Von Boltenstern of the 29th (mot.) division. The artillery of the 137th regiment replaced the 29th artillery regiment. On a logistical scale they had pulled it off, however, there was a lack of ammunition and the solders of the 137th ID were exhausted.

A Russian Kv-1 tank

Desná-Jelnja Arch: 'The Infantry Barely Fought'

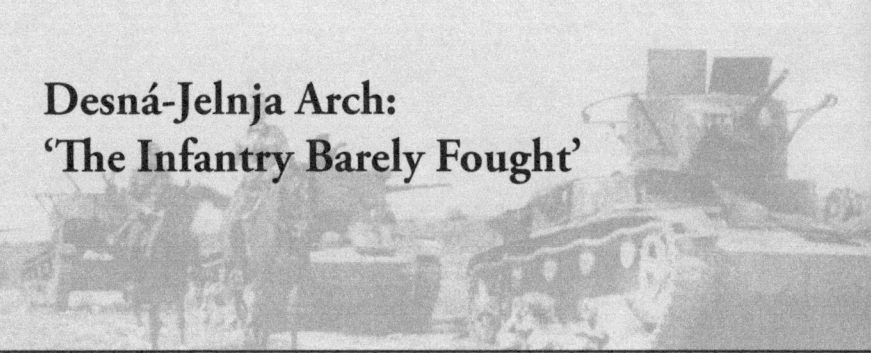

The lack of physical fitness led to new problems. The division commander, general Bergmann had deployed his battalions, however as soon as they were replaced, interventions occurred. Repeatedly the Rus-

A prelude to *'Barbarossa'*, a defeated Polish 7tp-tank, 1939

A train station at Smolensk. Russian tanks fall into German hands

sians took the initiative and chose to attack in the night. At Desná and Roslavl heavy fighting erupted in the early days of August 1941. It became so dangerous that Bergmann was forced to ask the replaced 29th division for help. Naturally this led to irritation, which became clear from Guderian's remarks at Roslawl. 'The infantry corps assigned to me, which until now barely fought against the Russians, had to get used to my methods of attack'. The infantry felt the same way, and after the fights at Roslawl, the 137th ID counted another 400 dead and injured soldiers. The armored units, however, easily recovered from the losses. Von Kluge voiced his concerns to Guderian as he stated that 'your operations are always at risk'. That indeed the wishes of the armory towards

Anti-aircraft guns on a sled

the infantry weren't always reasonable became evident after the command given to the 137th ID on August 5. Guderian made it clear he expected the division to reach the river Desná that day. However, at the time the division was fighting on three fronts at once, with a front line of 34 miles (which was very long), making a hasty operation towards the bridges over the Desná perhaps a bit too ambitious. In addition, as it turned out the bridges had already been blown up. A forced breach towards the supposed bridges would serve no purpose whatsoever. Bergmann was right in saving the troops to some extent. The

An operation at the Pripyat swamps

so-called Desná defense, at Jelnja, became the focus at the front. Something remarkable occurred here, which was typical to many Soviet-attacks. The Russians operated without any imagination and attacked at set times at the same place. Each time it came to brutal confrontations, however they all had the same results: a massacre amongst Soviet-attackers. This can be explained with the structure of command of the Red Army, where one proceeded on a very hierarchic scale where own initiative was not applauded. Soldiers blindly followed orders. All this was supported by iron discipline. Behind the front NKVD-troops

New tanks replace the 35 (t) and 38 (t) tanks

A shot down fighter plane

At the *'Rollbahn'* (the main marching route), a defeated light-weight Soviet tank

were continuously active (military police), to make sure no one deserted.

History often spoke of the armored troops

General Bergmann in conflict with the armored troops at the Desna-defense

The front at the Jelnja-curve

The Red Army's Unimaginative Performances: Daily Assaults and – Massacres

The seriousness of the situation became evident during the Finnish-Russian war where, as we can read in Carl van Dyke's work, the armored troops were sent

Erich Hoeppner and Von Kluge, Russia, 'Heeresgruppe'

forward without infantry back-up, because the infantry hadn't received orders to attack yet. On the forest paths tanks without infantry did not stand a chance and whole units drove towards their deaths. The most terrible event occurred during operation 'March' in 1942. Historian David M. Glantz typified this as 'Zjoekows biggest defeat'. This operation was in fact one close to 'Uranus' (the operations at Stalingrad), however, it has been completely forgotten. Between November and December of 1942 the Red army lost more than 200.000 soldiers during a blind assault, mostly at the so-called Vazuza-bridgehead.

Soviet prisoners of wars

The Red Army's Unimaginative Performances: Daily assaults and – Massacres

Most of these soldiers belonged to the infantry. For instance, the 20th, 31st, and 29th lost approximately 80% of their original occupancy, and the 26th Guard Infantry division of the Red Army had only 497 men left, of the 7.000 men with which they started the attack. However, not only soldiers paid the price. The Red Army's 2nd Guard Cavalry corps had 1.200 horses at its disposal, but lost 1.150. A similar percentage was seen during the German retreat at the fortress Sevastopol on the Crimea in 1944. At that point there was no room for the horses with which

Soviet cavalry. The 2nd Guard Cavalry corps lost approximately 1150 of its horses during operation 'Uranus'

the German army retreated and sought cover in the fortress. Approximately 27.000 horses were shot to prevent them from falling in Russian hands. Most of them were shot by Romanian troops and thrown off cliffs into the ocean. It was a horrible tragedy. Similar to the battle at Jelnja, was the fight for the Voronezh-Don-defense in 1942, 1943. Here the Red Army excelled once again with their unimaginative attacks against units of the 340th, 26th, 82nd, 68th, and 377th ID. Voronezh had been cleared, and at the ghost town endless repercussions took place. The

A light-weight Russian tank, Bt-5

fights at Jelnja belonged to the heaviest fights during the war.

The war at the eastern front was a world in itself. With the previous words we have tried to highlight some of the lesser known facts. Here attention was paid to political and military subjects and especially the overlaps in between. Without pretending to be complete, it is of the utmost importance for western readers to know the size and nature of the war in the east, where the Holocaust – the death by bullets – as well as the military actions, reached unequaled scales. In the works cited list the reader will find additional

A killed Soviet soldier still holding the hand grenade

The Red Army's Unimaginative Performances: Daily assaults and – Massacres

new sources, also within these series which will be expanded regularly.

Soviet prisoners of war are put to work by the *'Wehrmacht'*. A private picture taken by a German soldier

General Zjoekov, Stalingrad's hero. However, his defeat during operation 'Uranus' remained unknown

Works Cited:

Baschin, J., *Der Panzerkampfwagen 35 (t)*. (Friedland 2001)

Bongartz, H., *Luftmacht Deutschland. Aufstieg, Kampf und Sieg.* (Essen 1941)

Chamberlain, P./Ellis, C., *German tanks & Fighting vehicles of World War II*. (London 1976)

Cüppers, M., *Wegbereiter der Shoa. Die Waffen-SS, der Kommandostab Reichsführer SS und die Judenvernichtung 1939-1945.* (Darmstadt 2011)

Dyke, C. van., *The Soviet Invasion of Finland 1939-1940.* (Portland 1997)

Hasenclever,J., *Wehrmacht und Besatzungspolitik in der Sowjetunion. Die Befehlshaber der rückwärtigen Heeresgebiete 1941-1943.* (Paderborn 2010)

Hoffmann,J., *Stalins Vernichtungskrieg 1941-1945. Planung, Ausführung und Dokumentation.* (München 2000)

Mayer-Detring,W., *Die 137. Infanterie-Division im Mittelabschnitt der Ostfront.* (Eggolsheim)

Musial, B., *Kampfplatz Deutschland. Stalins Kriegspläne gegen den Westen.* (Berlin 2010)

Musial,B., *Stalins Beutezug. Der Plünderung Deutschlands und der Aufstieg der Sowjetunion zur Weltmacht.* (München 2011)

Paul,W., *Brennpunkte. Die Geschichte der 6.Panzerdivision (1.leichte) 1937-1945.* (Osnabrück 1984)

Pierik,P., *Krim. Bestorming-belegering-verovering-bezetting en moord.* (Soesterberg 2014)

Pierik,P., *De geopolitiek van het Derde Rijk* (Soesterberg 2012)

Richter, K./C., *Die Geschichte der deutschen Kavallerie 1919-1945.* (Stuttgart 1994)

Scheibert,H., *Die 6.Panzer-Division 1937-1945. Bewaffnung, Einsätze, Männer.* (Dorheim 1975)

Senger und Etterlin, F.M.von., *Die deutsche Panzer 1926-1945.* (Bonn 1999)

SS-Kavallerie im Osten. (Kiel 2006)

Toliver, R.F./Trevor, C.J., *Holt Hartmann vom Himmel!* (Stuttgart 1972)

Woronesch/Don Stellung 1942/43. Ausgewählte Dokumente.